Hedgehogs

by Kari Schuetz

BLASTOFF! READERS

BELLWETHER MEDIA • MINNEAPOLIS, MN

Note to Librarians, Teachers, and Parents:

Blastoff! Readers are carefully developed by literacy experts and combine standards-based content with developmentally appropriate text.

Level 1 provides the most support through repetition of high-frequency words, light text, predictable sentence patterns, and strong visual support.

Level 2 offers early readers a bit more challenge through varied simple sentences, increased text load, and less repetition of high-frequency words.

Level 3 advances early-fluent readers toward fluency through increased text and concept load, less reliance on visuals, longer sentences, and more literary language.

Level 4 builds reading stamina by providing more text per page, increased use of punctuation, greater variation in sentence patterns, and increasingly challenging vocabulary.

Level 5 encourages children to move from "learning to read" to "reading to learn" by providing even more text, varied writing styles, and less familiar topics.

Whichever book is right for your reader, Blastoff! Readers are the perfect books to build confidence and encourage a love of reading that will last a lifetime!

This edition first published in 2013 by Bellwether Media, Inc.

No part of this publication may be reproduced in whole or in part without written permission of the publisher. For information regarding permission, write to Bellwether Media, Inc., Attention: Permissions Department, 5357 Penn Avenue South, Minneapolis, MN 55419.

Library of Congress Cataloging-in-Publication Data
Schuetz, Kari.
 Hedgehogs / by Kari Schuetz.
   p. cm. – (Blastoff! readers: animal safari)
 Audience: 4-8.
 Audience: K to grade 3.
 Summary: "Developed by literacy experts for students in kindergarten through grade three, this book introduces hedgehogs to young readers through leveled text and related photos"– Provided by publisher.
 Includes bibliographical references and index.
 ISBN 978-1-60014-863-7 (hardcover : alk. paper)
 1. Hedgehogs–Juvenile literature. I. Title.
 QL737.E753S38 2013
 599.33'2–dc23   2012031524

Printed in the United States of America, North Mankato, MN.

Contents

What Are Hedgehogs?

Hedgehogs are small **mammals** with pointed **snouts**. They have **quills** on their backs.

Adult hedgehogs have long, sharp quills. **Hoglets** are born with short, soft ones.

hoglet

7

Hedgehogs live in forests, deserts, and **savannahs**.

Hedgehogs sleep during the day. They cuddle up in nests or **burrows**.

Eating

Hedgehogs search
for food at night.
They dig for food
with their snouts
and claws.

Their favorite meal is **insects**. They also eat worms, snails, and frogs.

Some hedgehogs eat snakes. Their quills protect them from bites.

Staying Safe

Hedgehogs can be **prey** for foxes and badgers. They curl into tight balls to stay safe.

They raise
their quills to
fight these
predators.
Ouch!

Glossary

burrows—holes or tunnels in the ground

hoglets—baby hedgehogs

insects—small animals with six legs and hard outer bodies; an insect's body is divided into three parts.

mammals—warm-blooded animals that have backbones and feed their young milk

predators—animals that hunt other animals for food

prey—animals that are hunted by other animals for food

quills—sharp spines

savannahs—grasslands with scattered trees

snouts—the noses and mouths of some animals

To Learn More

AT THE LIBRARY

Brett, Jan. *Hedgie's Surprise*. New York, N.Y.: Scholastic, 2001.

Dunn, Mary R. *Hedgehogs*. Mankato, Minn.: Capstone Press, 2011.

Scamell, Ragnhild. *Ouch!* Intercourse, Pa.: Good Books, 2006.

ON THE WEB

Learning more about hedgehogs is as easy as 1, 2, 3.

1. Go to www.factsurfer.com.

2. Enter "hedgehogs" into the search box.

3. Click the "Surf" button and you will see a list of related Web sites.

With factsurfer.com, finding more information is just a click away.

Index

The images in this book are reproduced through the courtesy of: Juan Martinez, front cover, pp. 7 (small), 9 (right), 11, 15 (left, middle, right); NHPA/SuperStock, p. 5; Juniors/SuperStock, p. 7; Lenartowski/Age Fotostock, pp. 9, 13; Piotr Krzeslak, p. 9 (left); Giancarlo Gagliardi, p. 9 (middle); Dietmar Nill/naturepl.com, p. 15; Albert Visage/Minden Pictures, p. 17; Age Fotostock/SuperStock, p. 19; Frederic Desmette/Biosphoto, p. 21.